DISCARD

Passover

Buddy BOOKS
Holidays

ABDO
Publishing Company

A Buddy Book
by
Julie Murray

VISIT US AT
www.abdopublishing.com

Published by ABDO Publishing Company, 8000 West 78th Street, Edina, Minnesota 55439.

Printed in the United States of America, North Mankato, Minnesota.
052011
092011

 PRINTED ON RECYCLED PAPER

Coordinating Series Editor: Rochelle Baltzer
Editor: Sarah Tieck
Contributing Editors: Megan M. Gunderson, BreAnn Rumsch, Marcia Zappa
Graphic Design: Denise Esner
Cover Photograph: *Thinkstock*: Jupiterimages.
Interior Photographs/Illustrations: *Alamy*: PhotoStock-Isreal (p. 15); *Getty Images*: Fuse (p. 19), Jupiterimages (p. 21), Bill Pugliano (p. 5); *Glow Images*: Stapleton Historical Collection (pp. 7, 9); *iStockphoto*: ©iStockphoto.com/PapaBear (p. 22), ©iStockphoto.com/SychuginaElena (p. 13); ©photolibrary.com (p. 11); *Shutterstock*: Noam Armann (p. 13), Ella's Design (p. 11), MG photos (p. 17).

Library of Congress Cataloging-in-Publication Data

Murray, Julie, 1969-
 Passover / Julie Murray.
   p. cm. -- (Holidays)
 ISBN 978-1-61783-040-2
 1. Passover--Juvenile literature. I. Title.
 BM695.P3P37 2011
 296.4'37--dc22
                                    2011002286

Table of Contents

What Is Passover?

Passover is an important Jewish holiday. It begins every year in March or April and lasts up to eight days. Its dates change from year to year. Passover celebrates how ancient Jews were freed from slavery in Egypt.

Passover is a time when Jews share their history. During Passover, they retell important stories from long ago.

The First Passover

Long ago, Jews were slaves in Egypt. Pharaoh forced them to work hard in the hot sun. They built things with heavy bricks and mortar.

A Jew named Moses told Pharaoh, "Let my people go." But, Pharaoh refused. So, God sent ten plagues to make him obey.

During the plagues, Egyptian animals got sick and died. Water turned to blood. And, insects ate crops that belonged to the Egyptians.

The tenth plague killed the oldest son in each Egyptian family. But, death passed over the Jewish houses. God had told the Jews to kill lambs and put blood on their doorposts. This kept Jewish children safe.

After this, Pharaoh freed the Jews. The Jews quickly left Egypt. As they were leaving, Pharaoh changed his mind. He sent soldiers after them.

But, the Jews made it safely to freedom. Today, this story is told each year during Passover.

God helped Moses part the sea so Jews could escape. The water closed on the soldiers following them.

Getting Ready

According to the Torah, Jews must follow special rules during Passover week. One rule says Jews may not eat, use, or have any bread products that have risen. They only eat matzo. Matzo is flat bread that has not risen.

Eating matzo helps Jews remember how quickly the ancient Jews escaped Egypt. They left so fast, there was no time for their bread to rise! Instead, they ate matzo.

Many Jews prepare their homes and businesses for Passover. They cook and clean. They also remove all risen bread products.

Matzo is crunchy and flat like a cracker.

At the Heart

Seder (SAY-duhr) dinner is the heart of Passover. It usually takes place on the first and second nights of Passover. Jewish families gather together for this meal.

The table is set for Seder with a special plate. A book called the Haggadah (huh-GAH-duh) is at each place. Stories, blessings, and songs for Seder are in it.

Seder has 15 steps. They include reading the Haggadah and washing hands.

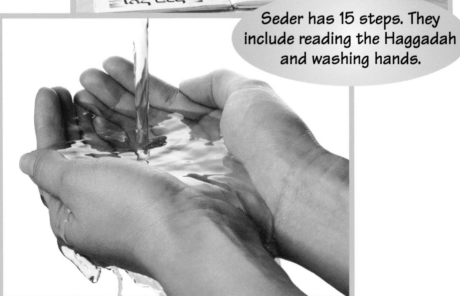

The youngest child has an important job at Seder dinner. He or she asks four questions from the Haggadah. Together, everyone reads the answers out loud. The answers help them know the meaning of Passover.

At some Seder dinners, all the children ask the four questions together.

Special Symbols

Items in the Seder dinner are symbols. They help tell the Passover story.

During Seder, Jews dip a green vegetable in salty water and eat it. Some believe the vegetable stands for human bodies or the lowly beginnings of the Jews. The salty water symbolizes the tears of the slaves.

As the Passover story is told, the food on the Seder plate is eaten or removed. This is done in a certain order.

To remember slavery's bitterness, Jews eat bitter vegetables or herbs. To remember mortar, they eat a mixture of fruit and nuts. A cooked egg and a lamb bone symbolize ancient offerings.

During the meal, a piece of matzo is broken. Part is set aside for dessert. It is called the afikomen (ah-fih-KOH-muhn). In some families, an adult hides it for children to find at the end of the meal.

Some families give a prize to the child who finds the afikomen!

Passover Today

Jews have celebrated Passover for thousands of years. But, it hasn't always been easy. During World War II, Jews were treated very badly. To stay safe, they honored Passover in secret.

Today, many Jewish families celebrate Passover openly in their homes. Most are able to safely share their beliefs. By doing this, they remember the ancient Jews.

Throughout Seder dinner,
people say blessings.

Passover Facts

- During Seder dinner, people drink four glasses of wine or grape juice.

- Jews pour an extra glass of wine or grape juice during Seder. This is for the Jewish **prophet** Elijah. Some believe he will appear at a future Seder dinner.

- Ancient Jews spoke in a language called Hebrew. The Hebrew word for Passover is Pesach (PAY-sahk). Hebrew is still important to modern Jews.

The Hebrew alphabet has 22 letters. Hebrew writing looks very different from English.

Important Words

celebrate to observe a holiday with special events.

mortar something used in building to hold bricks or stones together.

Pharaoh (FEHR-oh) the ruler of ancient Egypt.

plague (PLAYG) a disease or event that causes deaths or harm to many.

prophet (PRAH-fuht) someone who brings messages to others from a god.

slaves people bought and sold as property. Slavery is the act of owning slaves.

symbol (SIHM-buhl) an object or mark that stands for an idea. To symbolize is to act as a symbol.

Torah the Hebrew religious teachings and laws.

World War II a war fought in Europe, Asia, and Africa from 1939 to 1945.

Web Sites

To learn more about Passover,

visit ABDO Publishing Company online. Web sites about Passover are featured on our Book Links page. These links are routinely monitored and updated to provide the most current information available.

www.abdopublishing.com

Index